X-Sports
MOUNTAINBOARDING

BY ERIC PRESZLER

CONSULTANT:
DON BAKER
DIRTHEADS.COM

Capstone
press

Mankato, Minnesota

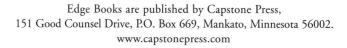

Edge Books are published by Capstone Press,
151 Good Counsel Drive, P.O. Box 669, Mankato, Minnesota 56002.
www.capstonepress.com

Library of Congress Cataloging-in-Publication Data
Preszler, Eric.
    Mountainboarding / by Eric Preszler.
    p. cm.—(Edge books. X-sports)
    Includes bibliographical references and index.
    ISBN 0-7368-3781-7 (hardcover)
    1. Mountainboarding—Juvenile literature. I. Title. II. Series.
GV859.762.P74 2005
796.93—dc22   2004022055

Summary: Introduces the sport of mountainboarding, including history, equipment, and
some popular mountainboarding parks.

Editorial Credits
Connie Colwell Miller, editor; Jason Knudson, set designer; Enoch Peterson and
    Linda Clavel, book designers; Jason D. Miller, illustrator; Jo Miller, photo
    researcher; Scott Thoms, photo editor

Photo Credits
Aurora/Scott Warren, 14
Corbis/Duomo, 11, 13; Eric Perlman, 15; Jamie Budge, 9, 18
Dirtheads.com/Kevin Delaney, cover, 21, 23
Image Ideas Inc., cover (background)
Mark Toms, 17
MBS Mountainboards/Geoff Ragatz, 7, 27; Jason Lee, 29; Steve Bonini, 20;
    Tom Kimmell, 5
Photodisc, 6

1 2 3 4 5 6 10 09 08 07 06 05

TABLE OF CONTENTS

CHAPTER 1

MOUNTAINBOARDING

Blood and dirt cover the mountainboarder's elbow. It's a hot summer day, and a group of fans waits at the bottom of a ski run. Mud, dirt, and rocks cover the slope.

The rider hops on his board for one last try. He pushes against the dirt with one foot to gain speed. The rider steers his board down the ski slope and around the muddy curves. The board's tires spin faster and faster.

He jumps over large rocks and ruts. He almost falls off his board when he hits a bump. But the rider catches his balance just in time. He reaches the bottom of the slope without falling once. The fans cheer.

LEARN ABOUT:

- Summer snowboarding
- Lee and McConnell
- MountainBoard Sports Company

4

Mountainboarders ride over large rocks and ruts.

Many mountainboarders go snowboarding in the winter.

MOUNTAINBOARDING HISTORY

Mountainboarding is becoming a popular extreme sport. The sport combines snowboarding, skateboarding, and dirt bike racing. Mountainboarding is sometimes called all-terrain boarding or dirt surfing.

Jason Lee and Patrick McConnell invented mountainboarding in 1993 in California. These friends enjoyed snowboarding and skiing. They wanted to practice on the slopes in the summer.

Lee and McConnell replaced a skateboard's wheels with large rubber tires. They rode this board down hills. They called it a mountainboard.

In 1993, Lee and McConnell started the MountainBoard Sports Company in Colorado Springs, Colorado. By 2004, the company was making about 20,000 boards a year.

Mountainboarding has caught on with about 1 million people around the world. Many fans of snowboarding and skateboarding enjoy mountainboarding. The fast pace of the sport gives them a new challenge.

Mountainboarders enjoy the fast pace and thrills of their sport.

CHAPTER 2

MOUNTAINBOARDING GEAR

Mountainboarders need a variety of gear to enjoy their sport safely. Riders need a mountainboard, helmet, and other equipment.

MOUNTAINBOARDS

Every mountainboarder needs a good board. Most mountainboards are made of wood or fiberglass. They are 3 to 4 feet (.9 to 1.2 meters) long. They weigh 14 to 17 pounds (6.4 to 7.8 kilograms).

Most mountainboards have bindings. Straps or bars hold riders' feet in place. Bindings help riders control the movements of their boards.

LEARN ABOUT:

- Bindings and brakes
- Tires and air pressure
- Staying safe

Mountainboards have bindings
to hold riders' feet in place.

Some mountainboards have brakes. Mountainboards travel quickly down hills. Beginning mountainboarders need brakes to help them stop.

Some mountainboarders use a board leash. This rope connects the board to the rider's ankle or wrist. The leash keeps the board nearby in case the rider crashes.

TIRES

Most mountainboards have four rubber tires. Tires vary in size and style. Most tires are 8 to 12 inches (20 to 30 centimeters) across. The tires need to be large enough to roll over mud, dirt, and rocks.

The amount of air in a mountainboard tire is called air pressure. High air pressure causes a board to travel fast. Lower air pressure makes a board travel more slowly. Beginning riders usually release some air from their tires. Lower air pressure helps beginners ride more slowly while they learn.

Mountainboard tires need to be large enough to help riders move through mud.

SAFETY EQUIPMENT

Mountainboarding can be dangerous. Even experienced riders crash. They often get cuts and bruises. Some even break bones.

A helmet is the most important piece of safety equipment. Head injuries are very serious. Mountainboarders should wear a fitted helmet whenever they ride. Mountainboarding helmets are lightweight. They cover the top and back of the rider's head.

Other safety equipment can help prevent injuries. Knee, elbow, and wrist pads help protect riders from broken bones, cuts, and bruises. Long pants, shirts, and gloves protect the skin. Goggles shield riders' eyes from flying dirt and rocks.

Fitted helmets protect mountainboarders from serious head injuries.

13

Many boarders also wear hip and backside armor made of cloth and foam. This gear protects riders when they fall.

A first aid kit is another important item for mountainboarders. This case is filled with bandages, cream for cuts and scrapes, and other equipment.

Even the most experienced riders sometimes crash.

Proper safety gear can help mountainboarders prevent injury.

EDGE FACT

When a boarder rides with the right foot forward instead of the left, it's called "goofy-footed."

CHAPTER 3

MOUNTAINBOARDING TRICKS

Mountainboarders use their boards in different ways. Riders can use their mountainboards to travel on flat land. They also ride down ski slopes, hills, and mountains. Riders even perform exciting tricks like jumps and flips.

Mountainboarding tricks are similar to snowboarding and skateboarding tricks. Riders perform their tricks while jumping in the air with their boards.

Mountainboarding tricks require a great deal of work. Riders spend hours practicing new moves. They perform tricks off jumps, over rocks, and on flat land.

LEARN ABOUT:

- The indy grab
- The Canadian Bacon Air
- The Rodeo Flip

Mountainboarders perform exciting tricks for fans.

Grabs are tricks that many new mountainboarders can do.

BASIC TRICKS

The indy grab is a beginning trick. In the air, riders grab the toe edge of the board. Many riders also hold their free hand up in the air.

The nose roll is another trick beginners can learn. Boards must have bindings for this trick. Riders go forward slowly. They shift their weight to the front, or nose, of the board. They then turn their shoulders and swing their back foot forward. The board swings around to complete the trick.

EDGE FACT

Ross Baker from Reno, Nevada, is the youngest national mountainboard competitor. He won many competitions when he was 11 years old.

INTERMEDIATE TRICKS

The backswing is a more difficult trick to learn. In the air, a rider grabs the board's nose. The rider then slips the front foot out of the binding. The rider swings the front foot back toward the other foot. To land, the rider slips the front foot back on the board or in the binding.

Mountainboarders perform tricks in rocky and mountainous locations.

Grabbing part of the board with one hand is a part of many mountainboarding tricks.

The Canadian Bacon Air is another difficult trick. In this trick, the rider reaches behind the back leg and grabs the board between the bindings. The rider then straightens out the front leg.

ADVANCED TRICKS

The 360 Flying Squirrel Air is an advanced trick. In this trick, riders spin around in a complete circle while in the air. The riders bend their knees and grab the edge of the board with both hands.

Other advanced tricks involve difficult spins and flips. The Rodeo Flip involves spinning around in a complete circle, plus spinning in another half circle.

Pro mountainboarders can win money by performing advanced tricks in competitions. They combine huge jumps with spins and grabs to impress judges and win titles. In 2003, one mountainboarder won $3,000 for a trick performed at the first U.S. Open Mountainboard Championships.

Advanced mountainboard tricks involve spins and flips.

HOW TO DO AN INDY GRAB

1. The rider travels straight toward a jump or hill.

2. As the rider travels off the edge of the jump or hill, the rider brings the legs up toward the body.

3. The rider grabs the board on the toe edge between the feet. At the same time, the rider sticks one arm in the air.

4. The rider lets go of the board and begins to straighten both legs to land.

CHAPTER 4

MOUNTAINBOARDING PARKS

Mountainboarders practice their sport almost anywhere they can. Many riders practice on hills and mountains near their homes. Some people also mountainboard at skiing and snowboarding parks. These parks include Snowmass Village Resort. The Holler is a park built just for mountainboarding.

THE HOLLER

Mountainboarders practice their skills at the Holler Mountainboard Park. Mountainboarder Justin Rhodes built this park in Fletcher, North Carolina. The Holler has mountainboarding courses, jumps, rails, and a training trampoline.

LEARN ABOUT:

- The Holler's foam pit
- Competitions
- Future of mountainboarding

The Holler is a place for mountainboarders to practice and compete.

The park is well-known for its foam pit. This wooden training pit is filled with foam padding. The pit allows riders to practice difficult moves with little risk of injury.

Many mountainboarders can practice their sport at the Holler. Beginning mountainboarders can take classes and learn new skills. Advanced riders can participate in one of the events or competitions held at the Holler. In 2004, The RIDE Tour Championship was held at the Holler. This championship is a national mountainboarding competition.

SNOWMASS VILLAGE RESORT

Mountainboarders also practice their moves at Snowmass Village Resort. This ski resort in Aspen, Colorado, is famous for its skiing and snowboarding. Today, people can also mountainboard at Snowmass.

Snowmass hosted the first U.S. Open Mountainboard Championships in 2003. The resort hosted this mountainboarding competition again in 2004.

Mountainboarding is still a new sport. Athletes all over the world are working to increase the sport's popularity.

In 2003, the U.S. Open Mountainboard Championships were held at Snowmass.

GLOSSARY

air pressure (AIR PRESH-ur)—the amount of air in a mountainboard tire; tires with less air in them slow down the speed of the board.

armor (AR-mur)—strong padded covering worn by mountainboarders to protect their bodies

bindings (BINDE-ingz)—straps that hold the riders' feet on the mountainboard

competition (kom-puh-TISH-uhn)—a contest between two or more people

fiberglass (FYE-bur-glass)—a strong material made from fine threads of glass; many mountainboards are made of fiberglass.

READ MORE

Freimuth, Jeri. *Extreme Skateboarding Moves.* Behind the Moves. Mankato, Minn.: Capstone Press, 2001.

Herran, Joe. *Snowboarding.* Action Sports. Philadelphia: Chelsea House, 2003.

INTERNET SITES

FactHound offers a safe, fun way to find Internet sites related to this book. All of the sites on FactHound have been researched by our staff.

Here's how:

1. Visit *www.facthound.com*
2. Type in this special code **0736837817** for age-appropriate sites. Or enter a search word related to this book for a more general search.
3. Click on the **Fetch It** button.

FactHound will fetch the best sites for you!

INDEX